A *LifeGuide*® Bible Study

CHRISTIAN BELIEFS

12 studies
for individuals or groups

Stephen Eyre

With Notes for Leaders

IVP Connect
An imprint of InterVarsity Press
Downers Grove, Illinois

InterVarsity Press
P.O. Box 1400, Downers Grove, IL 60515-1426
World Wide Web: www.ivpress.com
E-mail: mail@ivpress.com

InterVarsity Press® is the book-publishing division of InterVarsity Christian Fellowship/USA®, a student
movement active on campus at hundreds of universities, colleges and schools of nursing in the United
States of America, and a member movement of the International Fellowship of Evangelical Students. For
information about local and regional activities, write Public Relations Dept., InterVarsity Christian
Fellowship/USA, 6400 Schroeder Rd., P.O. Box 7895, Madison, WI 53707-7895, or visit the IVCF website
at <www.intervarsity.org>.

LifeGuide® is a registered trademark of InterVarsity Christian Fellowship.

Cover photograph: Dennis Flaherty

ISBN-10: 0-8308-3061-8
ISBN-13: 978-0-8308-3061-9

Printed in the United States of America ∞

| P | 25 | 24 | 23 | 22 | 21 | 20 | 19 | 18 | 17 | 16 | 15 | 14 | 13 | 12 | 11 | 10 | 9 | 8 | 7 | 6 |
| Y | 23 | 22 | 21 | 20 | 19 | 18 | 17 | 16 | 15 | 14 | 13 | 12 | 11 | 10 | 09 | 08 | 07 | 06 |

Contents

HOW GOD SAVES US

THE CHURCH: GOD'S HOLY PEOPLE

THE LAST THINGS

Getting the Most
Out of *Christian Beliefs*

As a new Christian in college, I wanted to learn all about the Christian faith through teaching, sermons and Bible study. I soon discovered, however, that many Bible studies and sermons left me both confused and frustrated. I had trouble putting all the pieces together—especially since various denominations seemed to hold different and often conflicting views. I wanted an overview of the basic truths that Christians believe.

Later I found that while there have always been theological differences among Christians, there is a great deal that we have in common. C. S. Lewis called this common core of belief "mere Christianity." These common beliefs can be briefly summarized under six headings.

☐ *Revelation*. It refers not to the last book in the Bible but to how God makes himself known.

☐ *God*. What is he like? What can we know about him?

☐ *Human Nature*. What are we like? How are we to relate to God? What happened when we sinned?

☐ *Salvation*. What has God done to rescue us from sin?

☐ *The Church*. Jesus has called us to follow him together. What does he require of us?

☐ *The Last Things*. Jesus is coming back. How can we live in hopeful expectation?

These headings also provide the outline for this study guide.

A systematic study of our beliefs as Christians can provide many personal and practical benefits. First, Christian beliefs help us make sense of the world we live in. How can we explain the presence of both incredible beauty and ugliness in the world? Why do we see not only supreme goodness but also diabolical evil? A knowledge of basic Christian beliefs helps us wrestle with questions that have baffled people for centuries.

Second, Christian beliefs strengthen our identity in Christ. Our culture urges us to seek our identity in our possessions, our personal achievements or our career. Yet Scripture tells us our identity is not derived from these things. It depends not on how others see us, but on how God sees us. As we learn the essential beliefs of Christianity, we begin to discover who we really are.

Third, Christian beliefs not only guide our thinking but also direct our behavior. In our day we desperately need men and women of integrity, people who are living examples of biblical values. As we learn these essential values, the Holy Spirit gradually transforms us into the likeness of Christ himself. Christian beliefs build Christian character.

Finally, and most importantly, Christian beliefs help us draw near to God. As we look into the Scriptures, we come to know the Author of Scripture. Biblical truths become a window into the heart and mind of God.

In our day there is a wishy-washy relativism that masquerades as faith. "It doesn't matter what you believe, just as long as you believe." "All roads lead to God." "The important thing is to be sincere." If we know what we believe, we will resist such shallow claims. God is personal. He has told us about himself and what he requires of us. All the rich knowledge of God is expressed through our Christian beliefs.

If we approach the Scriptures with humility and a fervent heart, Christian beliefs can strengthen our faith and ignite our souls. At the end of the guide is a reading list with books that you could explore on each of the study topics. For a comprehensive overview of Christian doctrine you might want to check out *Know the Truth* by Bruce Milne, *Knowing Christianity* by J. I. Packer, *Theology for Ordinary People* by Bruce L. Shelley or *Foundations of the Christian Faith* by James Montgomery Boice.

Suggestions for Individual Study

1. As you begin each study, pray that God will speak to you through his Word.

2. Read the introduction to the study and respond to the personal reflection question or exercise. This is designed to help you focus on God and on the theme of the study.

3. Each study deals with a particular passage—so that you can delve into the author's meaning in that context. Read and reread the passage to be studied. If you are studying a book, it will be helpful to read through the entire book prior to the first study. The questions are written using the language of the New International Version, so you may wish to use that version of the Bible. The New Revised Standard Version is also recommended.

4. This is an inductive Bible study, designed to help you discover for yourself what Scripture is saying. The study includes three types of questions. *Observation* questions ask about the basic facts: who, what, when, where and how. *Interpretation* questions delve into the meaning of the passage. *Application* questions help you discover the implications of the text for growing in Christ. These three keys unlock the treasures of Scripture.

Write your answers to the questions in the spaces provided or in a personal journal. Writing can bring clarity and deeper understanding of yourself and of God's Word.

5. It might be good to have a Bible dictionary handy. Use it to look up any unfamiliar words, names or places.

6. Use the prayer suggestion to guide you in thanking God for what you have learned and to pray about the applications that have come to mind.

7. You may want to go on to the suggestion under "Now or Later," or you may want to use that idea for your next study.

Suggestions for Members of a Group Study

1. Come to the study prepared. Follow the suggestions for individual study mentioned above. You will find that careful preparation will greatly enrich your time spent in group discussion.

2. Be willing to participate in the discussion. The leader of your group will not be lecturing. Instead, he or she will be encouraging the members of the group to discuss what they have learned. The leader will be asking the questions that are found in this guide.

3. Stick to the topic being discussed. Your answers should be based on the verses which are the focus of the discussion and not on outside authorities such as commentaries or speakers. These studies focus on a particular passage of Scripture. Only rarely should you refer to other portions of the Bible. This allows for everyone to participate in in-depth study on equal ground.

4. Be sensitive to the other members of the group. Listen attentively when they describe what they have learned. You may be surprised by their insights! Each question assumes a variety of answers. Many questions do not have "right" answers, particularly questions that aim at meaning or application. Instead the questions push us to explore the passage more thoroughly.

When possible, link what you say to the comments of others. Also, be affirming whenever you can. This will encourage some of the more hesitant members of the group to participate.

5. Be careful not to dominate the discussion. We are sometimes so eager to express our thoughts that we leave too little opportunity for others to respond. By all means participate! But allow others to also.

6. Expect God to teach you through the passage being discussed and through the other members of the group. Pray that you will have an enjoyable and profitable time together, but also that as a result of the study you will find ways that you can take action individually and/or as a group.

7. Remember that anything said in the group is considered confidential and should not be discussed outside the group unless specific permission is given to do so.

8. If you are the group leader, you will find additional suggestions at the back of the guide.

1

God in the World & in the Word

Psalm 19

"I don't believe in God!" That was my declaration as a confused and angry teenager. However, I found my unbelief hard to maintain. My adolescent hungers weren't satisfied in the "normal" places like music, friends or school. But during my first year of college, God began to reveal himself to me in ways that I couldn't deny. After a year of his constant calling, I yielded.

GROUP DISCUSSION. C. S. Lewis writes, "Avoiding [God], in many times and places, has proved so difficult that a very large part of the human race has failed to achieve it." What influences and events have led you to faith in God?

PERSONAL REFLECTION. Both head and heart are required for a healthy relationship with God. Sit quietly and then consider: What do I feel toward God right now?

General revelation refers to the way that God makes his existence known in the world. *Special revelation* is the term for how God makes his will known to his people. Psalm 19 is a meditative reflection by the psalmist on both special and general revelation. *Read Psalm 19.*

1. How does the psalmist help us perceive the presence of the invisible God?

2. The psalmist views the world as we might view a work of art (v. 1). How does seeing the world in this way help us to appreciate God's glory?

3. The psalmist says the creation speaks in every language and in every corner of the world (v. 2). What can anyone in the world know about God through creation?

4. What are some things about God that can't be known through creation?

5. The sun gets special mention (vv. 4-6). How is God's glory particularly revealed in the sun?

6. Which aspects of creation have helped you learn the most about God and his glory? Explain.

7. In verses 7-14 the psalmist shifts his focus from the way God makes himself known in creation to the way he reveals himself in his law. What words does the psalmist use to describe God's law?

8. According to the psalmist, what are the benefits of knowing God's law?

What benefits have you received from God's law?

---

9. Why would reflecting on God's creation and his law cause David to think about his own responsibility before God (vv. 11-13)?

How do both nature and God's law bring up the idea of sin and our need of forgiveness?

---

10. God is a person who is making an effort to be known. What should you be willing to do to know him better?

Tell God that you want to know him better. Ask him to open your eyes to a sense of his presence and your mind to the understanding of his character.

Now or Later

The sense of God's presence is all around us, but for many reasons we are dull in our spiritual perception. Keep a record this week of every time that God comes to mind. At the end of the week review your notes and see if there are special actions or places that are a special means of God's presence in your life.

2

Knowing God

During my years as staff member with InterVarsity Christian Fellowship, I had the privilege of encountering many students who were not yet Christians. When talking to them about God, I frequently heard a common refrain: "My God is not like that."

Different religions are all around us—secularism, Buddhism, Hinduism, Islam—and every religion has its own set of beliefs about God. As Christians we believe in the God of Abraham, the God and Father of Jesus Christ. But who is he, and what is he like?

GROUP DISCUSSION. What are some common opinions that you run into about what God is like?

PERSONAL REFLECTION. A. W. Tozer wrote, "What comes into your mind when you think about God is the most important thing about you." Consider what comes into your mind when you think about God.

In this chapter Isaiah writes as though Judah's captivity in Babylon judgment is almost over. His comforting words present a dramatic portrait of God. *Read Isaiah 40:9-31.*

---

1. Some people have the idea that thinking about the character of God is abstract and not very practical. What might Isaiah say to that? (Draw from his proclamation of the good tidings of God, vv. 9-11.)

2. What do Isaiah's questions encourage us to ponder about God (vv. 12-14)?

3. Focus on verses 15-24. What encouraging insights about God does Isaiah's contrasting of God with the nations surrounding Israel lead to?

4. Isaiah prophesied in order to bring comfort to Israel as they were facing threats from other countries. What comfort do you receive from knowing God has power over the nations?

5. Isaiah exposes the foolishness of idolatry (vv. 18-24) in his day by comparing it to the power of the Creator God. What idols in our culture need to be exposed as foolish by the power of the Creator God?

6. Why is it that worshiping idols in any age and culture seems preferable to worshiping the living God?

7. Some people today view God as an uninvolved Creator who stands at a distance to watch his world. What does verse 26 reveal about God's involvement?

8. Classical theology describes the essential characteristics of God as eternal—God's existence which transcends time, infinite—unlimited by time or by space, omnipresent—present everywhere at all times, and omniscient—knowing everything that is happening everywhere. How many of these characteristics can you discover in verses 27 and 28?

9. Some people in Isaiah's time, not understanding these wonderful characteristics of God, complain that God doesn't know what is happening to them (vv. 27-28). What hope does Isaiah offer them (vv. 28-31)?

10. What does it personally and practically mean to you that God's knowledge is not limited by anything?

---

11. Those who know God look to him for help. Describe a time when the Lord renewed your strength or enabled you to soar on wings like an eagle.

Ask God to enable you to find strength for the challenges you face in his wonderful character and his personal commitment to you.

Now or Later

One famous description of God contained in the Westminster Shorter Catechism is this: "God is a Spirit, infinite, eternal and unchangeable in his being, wisdom, power, justice and love." Choose a characteristic of God mentioned in this definition for each day of the upcoming week. Reflectively ponder that characteristic throughout the day; consider why it's good that God is like that. Consider as well what you (and the world) would be missing if he weren't.

God is holy (Exodus 3:5-6; 19:23); God is good (Luke 18:19; Romans 8:28); God is omnipresent (Psalm 139:7-10); God is omniscient (1 John 3:20; Matthew 6:8) God is omnipotent (Matthew 19:26; Psalm 115:3); God is immutable—unchanging in his character (Malachi 3:6; James 1:17); God is perfect (Matthew 5:48); God is love (John 3:16; Romans 5:8; 1 John 4:10-11); God is forgiving and compassionate (Psalm 103:3-6; Exodus 3:7-8).

3

Jesus:
God with Us

John 1:1-18

Almost everyone believes *something* about Jesus. Some suggest that he was merely a great teacher. But as C. S. Lewis wrote, any serious look at the Gospels rules out that option. In fact, Lewis reduced our options to three words: *liar, lunatic* or *Lord*.

If Jesus knew he was not God but chose to deceive others anyway, then he was a liar. If he truly thought he was God but was self-deluded, then he was a lunatic. However, if Jesus was neither a liar nor a lunatic, then the third option is inescapable—he is Lord and has the right to be believed and obeyed.

GROUP DISCUSSION. What are some common opinions in your experience that people express about Jesus?

PERSONAL REFLECTION. What in your personal experience led you to believe in Jesus as Lord? What continues to affirm and confirm your faith that he is Lord?

Through their accounts of Jesus' teaching and actions, Matthew, Mark, Luke and John show us his divine character and the eternally saving work he achieved for us. In classic theology this is referred to as "the person and work of Jesus." The Gospel of John is the most explicit of all four Gospels in declaring Jesus' person and work in its opening verses. *Read John 1:1-18.*

---

1. John writes with images and metaphors, referring to Jesus as the *Word,* the *life* and the *light* (vv. 1-9). What do these images communicate about him?

---

2. How have you experienced Jesus as Word, life and light?

---

3. The opening words about the Word are not easy to comprehend (vv. 1-4). As we seek to unravel these puzzling words, we are confronted with our limited ability to comprehend God. How do you respond to the idea that the Word is both God and with God?

---

4. What actions that only God can do are attributed to the Word?

---

5. Why might these verses and others like them lead early Christian theologians to develop the doctrine of the Trinity—that there is one

God but three persons?

---

6. How does John's mention of light versus darkness prepare us to understand the outcome of Jesus' earthly ministry (vv. 5, 10-13)?

How does it help us understanding the subsequent course of Christianity through the march of two thousand years of history?

---

7. Not only is Jesus God, but he became a human (vv. 14-15). This is referred to in classic theology as the incarnation. Why might the incarnation be described as the ultimate miracle against which all other supernatural works of God pale in comparison?

---

8. How do these verses speak to the mistaken teaching that Jesus was merely an enlightened human with a highly developed "God consciousness"?

9. How do these verses speak to the mistaken teaching that Jesus became God because of the outstanding quality of the moral life that he lived?

---

10. John claims that they all received "one blessing after another" from Jesus (v. 16). What blessing does he refer to in verses 12 and 13?

What are some of the blessings you have received from your relationship with God through Jesus?

Thank God that he has come from heaven to enter the events of your life.

Now or Later

The privilege of becoming children of God is given to those who believe in the name of Jesus. Perhaps you could enter more fully into the emotional knowledge of this reality by picturing yourself as a child sitting in the lap of God as your heavenly parent. Sit there for a while and enjoy the care and security of his loving presence. After you have spent time in his presence, make a note of how it affected you.

For further study on God as Trinity:
☐ The Father is God: 1 Corinthians 8:6; John 5:23-24, 26; 8:54
☐ The Son is God: John 8:58-59; Colossians 1:15-19; 2:9
☐ The Holy Spirit is God: Psalm 139:7; Acts 5:3-4; Hebrews 9:14.

4

The Holy Spirit

While a theological graduate student, I began to explore the work of the Holy Spirit. I attended a seminary that taught that the gifts of the Spirit and supernatural manifestations had ceased at the end of the first century. However, I had friends involved in the charismatic movement who assured me from spiritual experience that this was not true. Who was I to believe?

GROUP DISCUSSION. Teaching about the Holy Spirit can be exciting for some and threatening for others. Some churches major on the work of the Holy Spirit and the gifts he brings. Other churches don't mention the Holy Spirit or spiritual gifts at all. What is your experience?

Why do you think that issues about the Holy Spirit can generate such emotion?

PERSONAL REFLECTION. In what ways are you aware of the work of the Spirit in your life? In what ways would you like to see the work of the Spirit in your life?

In pondering the differences I began to see that understanding the Holy Spirit begins not with spiritual gifts but with a personal connection with Jesus Christ. The foundational teaching on the Holy Spirit comes from Jesus as he prepares his disciples for a new spiritual connection with them that will bridge the gap between heaven and earth. *Read John 14:15-27.*

1. The night before his crucifixion Jesus tell his disciples that he is leaving them. They are troubled and fearful (14:1, 27). What does he say to calm their fears?

2. How do the titles Counselor and Spirit of truth (vv. 16-17) help them understand the nature of the One Jesus promised?

How have you experienced the Holy Spirit as a counselor and Spirit of truth?

3. What is the difference between a Christian's experience of the Holy Spirit and those of the world (vv. 17-18)?

4. From your experience, how can our daily concerns either dull or awaken our sense of the Spirit's presence?

5. Jesus promises that the relationship with the Spirit will be both *permanent* (v. 16) and *intimate* (v. 17). How does this address the anxiety of the disciples?

How might this address your spiritual anxieties?

6. Jesus promised to not leave us as orphans but continue with us through the Holy Spirit (v. 18). What is the relationship between the Jesus and the Holy Spirit?

How might this insight about the presence of Jesus and the Holy Spirit help provide a bridge between denominational differences on the Holy Spirit?

7. In the midst of anxiety Jesus promises peace (v. 27). What ministries of the Holy Spirit bring peace to Jesus' followers (vv. 25-27)?

Other places in the New Testament teach us that the Spirit works both in our hearts directly and through fellow Christians (Ephesians 1:17-18 and Ephesians 4:11-12). How have you experienced the ministry of the Spirit?

8. What differences are there between the Spirit-inspired peace of Jesus and that of the world (vv.25-27)?

9. As has been noted before, Christians believe that God is Trinity. There is one God existing in three persons—Father, Son and Holy Spirit. Based on this passage, how would you describe the relationship between Jesus, the Father and the Holy Spirit?

10. Throughout this passage, Jesus emphasizes the importance of keeping his commands in order to be in loving spiritual connection with him through the Holy Spirit (vv. 15-16, 21, 23). Describe the relationship between love and obedience.

---

11. What has this study revealed to you about your relationship with the Holy Spirit?

Pray the apostle Paul's prayer that ties the ministry of the Father, Son and Spirit together in the depth of our being: "For this reason I kneel before the Father, from whom his whole family in heaven and on earth derives its name. I pray that out of his glorious riches he may strengthen you with power through his Spirit in your inner being, so that Christ may dwell in your hearts through faith. And I pray that you, being rooted and established in love, may have power, together with all the saints, to grasp how wide and long and high and deep is the love of Christ, and to know this love that surpasses knowledge—that you may be filled to the measure of all the fullness of God" (Ephesians 3:14-19).

Now or Later

Ask God to refresh and renew your sense of the Spirit's work. Perhaps you could picture your heart as a large empty pool. Invite the Spirit to fill it. As you do make a note of what sort of insights and perspectives you gain about the Spirit's work inside of you.

Take time to read more about different aspects of the Spirit:
- [ ] the Spirit of God at creation (Genesis 1:1)
- [ ] the Spirit of God as God's presence (Psalm 139:7)
- [ ] the Spirit of God as holy (Isaiah 63:10)
- [ ] the Spirit of God as God's power (Zechariah 4:6)
- [ ] the Spirit of God as God (John 4:24)
- [ ] the Spirit of God as God's wisdom (John 14:26)

5

Our Identity & Dignity

Genesis 1:24—2:25

John Calvin, one of the early Reformers of the church, wrote in the opening pages of the *Institutes of the Christian Religion* that it wasn't clear which came first, a knowledge of ourselves or a knowledge of God our Creator. In any case, he wrote that our knowledge of self and God are important issues and inseparably intertwined.

GROUP DISCUSSION. Who are the people that have most shaped the way you perceive yourself?

PERSONAL REFLECTION. What makes you feel good about yourself? (Be honest!)

According to Genesis, we are made in the image of God. In this study we will consider what that means. *Read Genesis 1:24—2:25.*

---

1. We humans were created on the sixth day, along with the land animals. We are similar to them yet very different. What special privileges did God bestow on humanity (1:24-31)?

2. Compare the two accounts of the creation of the human race (1:26-30 and 2:4-25). What different emphasis is given in each account?

Together what do they teach us about ourselves?

3. How would you describe God's relationship with Adam (2:15-18)?

4. Imagine Adam beginning life with just the animals around him and no contact with God. How would his life have been different?

5. Like Adam, we too need to be on personal terms with God. How does knowing God make a difference in the way you live and think about yourself?

6. Adam was given complete freedom in the Garden except for access to the tree of the knowledge of good and evil (2:15-17). In what ways do you think placing that tree off-limits would have affected Adam?

What would Adam learn about God by this prohibition?

That if he did not lisen to God there would be a price to pay.
There would be rules and limits

7. What benefits have you received by the freedoms and restraints that God requires of you?

8. One of the special abilities that God gave to Adam, and all humans, is the ability to name (2:19). How does this naming ability set Adam, and all humans, apart from the rest of creation?

God gave humans the ability to think

9. As Adam is naming the animals, he discovers a need for companionship that isn't being met (1:18-25). How would you describe the intended relationship between Adam and Eve?

In what ways would Eve fill a need for companionship and help that neither God nor the animals filled?

10. God says that it isn't good for a man to be alone (1:18). From your experience, what is wrong with being alone?

How does feeling alone affect your sense of identity and self-worth?

---

11. Summarize the essentials of human identity that come from Genesis.

How might this passage provide insight for you to grow in your sense of dignity and self-worth?

Ask God to provide you with the relationships, responsibilities and personal connection with him that are essential for your well-being.

Now or Later

Since we are made in the image of God, we are very valuable. When we lose sight of this, we seek our values in what we own, what we do or the status others attribute to us. In order to gain a glimpse of your value to God, why not give him all your false sources of value and ask him to affirm you as his creation and his child. Picture yourself standing before him now with a box full of your trophies that stand for your efforts to achieve personal significance. Give them over to him and invite him to affirm you. After you have done this, make a note of how it affected you.

6

Our Identity
& Depravity

Genesis 3

Terrible themes recur in the evening news—pain, conflict, violence and corruption. Through the miracle of technology, we often see people inflict pain on other people. The victims of pain stretch from the cities we live in to the far reaches of the world. Every night there is a dreary inevitability about it. The themes are the same; only the names and circumstances change.

GROUP DISCUSSION. How can we explain this constant and universal pain and corruption? Is that just the way life is? Are they the result of evolution? natural causes? God? humanity? Explain.

PERSONAL REFLECTION. How do you feel when you hurt others because of your selfishness or thoughtlessness?

Genesis 3 is one of the most pivotal chapters in Scripture as we see the introduction of Christian understandings of the origin of human sin. *Read Genesis 3.*

---

1. If you were making a movie based on this passage, describe the music you would you use for the background.

2. The scene opens with a conversation between the serpent and the woman (vv. 1-5). How does the serpent raise doubts about God's motives?

3. The evil one approached Adam and Eve through the serpent. What disguises does he use today?

In what situations might he try to get us to question God's character and motives?

Hardship

4. Adam and Eve chose to disobey God. What do you think may have been going through their minds as they were eating the fruit (vv. 6-7)?

5. The first "fruit" of their disobedience was a sense of nakedness (v. 7). Why do you think they felt a need to make coverings for themselves?

6. Since Adam and Eve, all of us (except Jesus) have sinned. What "fig leaves" do we use to cover our own sins?

7. As God appears in the Garden (vv. 8-9), Adam and Eve are hiding in the bushes. How do we hide from God?

8. The Lord knows everything. Why then do you think he uses questions to investigate Adam and Eve's sin (vv. 9-13)?

To see how we answer

9. In response to sin, God delivers a curse. As the curse spreads throughout creation, what effects will it have on the human race (vv. 14-19)?

10. What hope does God provide even as he is delivering judgment (v. 15)?

11. Although his law is broken, God takes steps to extend his grace.

How does he give protection and grace to our sin-damaged race (vv. 21-24)?

12. There is no hope for us until we acknowledge that sin affects us—our relationships, self-image, actions and so on. How can we become more honest about ourselves and our sin?

13. This study and study five together cover the essentials of the Christian understanding of human nature. Summarize your understanding of human nature from Genesis 1—3.

The following prayer comes from churches with a strong liturgical tradition. Conclude your study time by praying this prayer or rephrasing it in a way that you feel comfortable: "Almighty God, my heavenly Father: I have sinned against you, through my own fault, in thought, and word and deed, and in what I have left undone. For the sake of your Son our Lord Jesus Christ, forgive me all my offenses and grant that I may serve you in newness of life, to the glory of your Name. Amen."

Now or Later

Invite God to take a tour of your inner life for the purpose of cleaning it out. Keep in mind that the purpose of this tour is not to condemn you but to cleanse you. As God walks through the corridors of your heart, let him see your self-centeredness, envy, anger, jealousy, bitterness and whatever else that God calls sin. Ask God to cleanse each sin with his transforming holiness and grace. After you have spent some time with God on this tour, make a note about how it affected you.

7

Deliverance
from Sin

Romans 3:9-31

Funny thing, *sin* is not a word that we use to describe wrongful behavior anymore. Somewhere in the twentieth century it dropped out of our daily speech. Yet, although the word *sin* is no longer used, the experience of guilt is as prevalent as ever.

GROUP DISCUSSION. What is the attitude of those around you—in your workplace and neighborhood—to the word *sin*?

Why do you think the word *sin* has fallen out of use in our daily vocabulary?

How does the contemporary attitude toward sin affect the way people think about Christianity?

PERSONAL REFLECTION. What sins do you struggle with, and how does the sense of being a sinner affect the way you feel about yourself?

God takes sin very seriously. That is why he has sent his Son to deliver us. The classic term to describe his initial work of deliverance is *justification*. The passage you are about to read is the most complete summary of justification in the New Testament. *Read Romans 3:9-20.*

---

1. Notice Paul's use of the words *all* and *no one* (vv. 9-12). How would you respond to those who claim that anyone who seeks God and does good will be acceptable to him?

2. Paul mentions several parts of the human body—throats, tongues, lips, mouths, feet and eyes (vv. 13-18). How do these paint a vivid picture of our spiritual and moral condition?

3. Why do you think we seldom see ourselves or those we know as fitting his description?

4. Jews tried to follow the Old Testament law as a means for overcoming sin. What was wrong with this (vv. 19-20)?

5. *Read Romans 3:21-31.* What hope does God offer those who are condemned, who have failed to become righteous by law?

What is God's part and what is our part in this righteousness?

6. What key words in verses 24-25 describe what God has done for us in Christ?

7. We are "justified freely" (v. 24), which means to be legally acquitted of all wrongdoing. What is free and what is costly about our justification?

8. The word *redemption* (v. 24) means to be bought from bondage to sin and freed into fellowship with God. How have you experienced deliverance from the slavery of avoiding and disobeying God?

9. The words "sacrifice of atonement" (v. 25) come from the temple sacrifices. How do you respond to the fact that Christ died the horrible death you deserved?

10. How does the righteousness from God demolish human pride (vv. 28-30)?

11. This passage shows all that God has done to restore our relationship with him. How do you feel toward God after reading this passage?

———————————————————————————————————————

12. Based on this passage, how would you explain to a non-Christian both the bad news about sin and the good news about Jesus Christ?

Thank God that he has delivered you from bondage to sin and delivered you into the kingdom of his Son, in which we have redemption from sin and great spiritual blessings both for this life and the life to come.

Now or Later

In the "Now or Later" section of the last study, you invited God to take a tour of your heart in order to expose some of the sins that were present. Review those sins that you became aware of. Now picture yourself standing before God in a courtroom with all those sins listed on legal document. Allow God to take that list and give it to Jesus Christ. Then listen to hear him say directly to you, "Not Guilty." What responses do you have?

Memorize the following classic definition of *justification:* "Justification is an act of God's free grace, by which he pardons all our sins, and accepts us as righteous in his sight, only for the righteousness of Christ imputed to us, and received by faith alone."

8

Freedom
to Be Holy

Addiction is slavery. We start out enjoying what later becomes a habit we can't break. Whether it is food, drugs or alcohol, there is a humiliating bondage to anything that controls us. Sin is an addiction. We may choose to do some action that we know to be wrong but seems to be pleasurable. We think we can stop whenever we choose but soon discover that we have desires that overcome our will to resist.

GROUP DISCUSSION. By the end of the first thousand years of Christian history, the church had identified seven deadly sins: envy, lust, sloth, pride, greed, gluttony and hate. What is "deadly" about each of these sins?

PERSONAL REFLECTION. Are there any of the seven deadly sins that you especially struggle with? How has God been working in your life to deliver you?

Once God has broken the power of sin through justification (study 7), he now leads us into the battle to stay free from sin. The classic term for this is *sanctification. Read Romans 8:1-17.*

1. What resounding good news does Paul declare to those who struggle with sin (vv. 1-4)?

2. How does deliverance from the condemnation of sin (v. 1) contribute to our deliverance from the act of sin?

3. God is not willing to leave us in a desperate state of condemnation. According to verses 1-17, how is the entire Trinity—Father, Son and Spirit—involved in our deliverance?

4. What contrasts does Paul make between those who live by the Spirit and those who live by their sinful nature (vv. 5-8)?

How can we know which description applies to us (v. 9)?

5. Paul states that Christians do not live according to the sinful nature (v. 4) and are not controlled by the sinful nature (v. 9). How does that fit with your experience? Explain.

6. According to Paul, what role does the mind play in a life of sin or a life of righteousness (vv. 5-8)?

How have you observed the role of the mind in your own combat with sin?

7. In living righteously, what is the difference between setting our minds on the Spirit and sheer willpower?

8. Explain in your own words the deep tension that exists between our body and our spirit (v. 10).

How will the Holy Spirit ultimately resolve that tension (v. 11)?

9. In light of what he has written, Paul states that we have an obligation (v. 12). What is our part and what is the Spirit's part in fulfilling that obligation (vv. 12-17)?

10. As you look back at this passage, how would you summarize the Spirit's work in our holiness?

_____

11. How can you cooperate with the Spirit as he keeps you free from the addiction to sin?

_____

12. Salvation could be described as both a definite act of God and an ongoing process. How do both *justification* (study 7) and *sanctification* work together to provide the way for living a holy life?

Thank God that he has delivered you from the condemnation of sin and the guilty conscious it produces. Ask that the Spirit might work in you the joy of being cleansed and forgiven

Now or Later

The following verses provide some further insight into the process of sanctification: Romans 6:4, 14; Ephesians 4:23-24; 2 Thessalonians 2:13; 2 Peter 1:3-11; 4:1-3.

9

The Best Is
Yet to Come

Romans 8:18-39

Whether your life has been relatively free of trouble or full of pain, there comes a point when you begin to feel there has to be more to this life—somewhere. Several years ago some commercials summarized a popular attitude: "You only go around once in life, so grab all the gusto you can get." Such an approach may sound attractive, but it isn't real. Ultimately we become frustrated as we find that some pleasures are beyond our reach or fail to live up to our expectations. The Bible presents a different perspective toward life. The good things we experience now are just a taste of what is to come. And the suffering we see and feel encourages us to live in anticipation of Christ's return.

GROUP DISCUSSION. When you think of life beyond the grave, what comes to mind?

PERSONAL REFLECTION. What experiences cause you to reflect on the limitations of this life?

God has delivered us from condemnation of sin through justification (study 7) and has given us the power to wrestle with sin by means of sanctification. In addition he wants us to anticipate and aspire to a greater experience of freedom in heaven on the other side of death.

This final state of God's victory over sin is, in classic Christian teaching, called *glorification*. *Read Romans 8:18-27.*

---

1. How does Paul describe the suffering that we (and the rest of creation) experience during the present time (vv. 18-25)?

---

2. What hope does Paul offer us in the midst of our suffering (vv. 18-25)?

How does the hope of future glory encourage you when you are suffering?

---

3. Paul speaks of waiting eagerly (v. 19) and waiting patiently (v. 25). How can these two ideas be reconciled?

---

4. How does the Spirit help us during our present sufferings, groanings and weakness (vv. 26-27)?

---

5. *Read Romans 8:28-39.* What is God's good purpose for us (vv. 29-30)?

What steps has God taken in order to fulfill that purpose?

6. Verse 28 is often misread. What is the difference between God "working in all things" (the better reading) and "causing all things" (the conventional misreading) for the good of those who love him?

7. Describe a time when the knowledge of God's loving control was a source of strength and comfort to you.

8. What guarantee do we have that God will fulfill his promises to us (vv. 31-34)?

9. Notice the dangers Paul says we face in this life (vv. 35-39). When have dangers and problems caused you to question God's love?

10. How do the powerful enemies that threaten us actually reveal the strength and depth of God's love (vv. 37-39)?

11. God's saving work is constant in our lives. How might the following sentences be a helpful summary of the classic Christian understanding of salvation encompassing justification, sanctification and glorification: I have been saved. I am being saved. I shall be saved.

12. How does your understanding of salvation as justification, sanctification and glorification affect the way you think and experience the Christian life?

Thank God for his love, present help and promises of future glory.

Now or Later

Picture yourself on the other side of death: you no longer struggle with sin, physical or emotional weakness, or any other problem. As you look back on your life, what do you see?

For further study read Philippians 1:21-22; 2:12-13; Hebrews 12:1-3; Revelation 4:1—5:14.

10

The Mission of the Church

Acts 2

I became disillusioned with the church during my high school years and dropped out. In college I resisted those from a church near the campus who sought to evangelize me. But even as I resisted, I saw something in that fellowship of believers that attracted me. I was drawn both to the Lord and the church.

GROUP DISCUSSION. What does your church do to participate in the mission of spreading the good news of salvation? What excites you about this?

Is there anything about the way your church is active in evangelism and missions that makes you uncomfortable? Explain.

PERSONAL REFLECTION. What motivates you to share your faith with others?

The church is God's mission base. In addition to saving us by means of justification, sanctification and glorification, God puts us together with others through whom he can continue to both enrich us and share with us the task of proclaiming his saving work to others who don't yet know him. *Read Acts 2:1-41.*

1. Looking over the whole chapter, what is the role of the three per-

sons of the Trinity in the mission of the church?

2. The events on the day of Pentecost begin to fulfill Jesus' promise in Acts 1:8 of church growth. What is there about this experience that lays the foundation for the church to be multicultural, multigenerational and multinational?

3. In what ways have you experienced the church as multicultural, multigenerational and multinational?

4. Peter and the disciples had been in hiding in fear and confusion after Jesus' crucifixion. How would you compare the attitude of Peter and the early church now?

5. The mission of the church is to proclaim the message "Jesus, whom you crucified, [is] both Lord and Christ" (v. 36). What reasons does Peter offer for believing that message (vv. 22-41)?

6. How does that first message about Jesus compare and contrast with the message the church proclaims today? (Give examples.)

---

7. Thousands responded to Peter's sermon (v. 22-39). Why do you think his message was so convincing to the people gathered in Jerusalem?

How convincing is that message in our culture today? Explain.

---

8. *Read Acts 2:42-47.* The church's mission and message created a fellowship. How would you describe that first fellowship of believers?

---

9. There were larger worship gatherings at the temple and smaller gatherings in homes (v. 46). Why are both important?

10. "The Lord added to their number daily" (v. 47). What is our role and what is God's role in the growth of the church?

11. What are the consequences of losing sight of our role or God's role in adding people to the church?

12. In what ways could your church or fellowship benefit from the example of the early church described in this chapter?

Ask God to give you the motivation to share in the task of spreading the good news of salvation to those who are like you and to those who are different from you.

Now or Later

Sharing the good news of Jesus with another in a way that leads to conversion is generally a process that takes place over a period of time rather than a one-time experience. What was the process by which you came to a saving faith in Jesus Christ?

How have you been involved in the process of sharing the faith with someone not yet a Christian?

11

The Community of the Church

The church is made up of all who call on the name of the Lord. We are *one* in Jesus Christ. We share a common-unity community. But the practice of Christian community is difficult. For example, I went to a Christian college that broke off from a denomination in the 1960s, which broke off from another denomination in the 1950s, which broke away from another denomination in the 1930s, which was part of a denomination that split in the 1850s.

GROUP DISCUSSION. Why do you think there are so many divisions in the church? How does the existence of so many denominations affect your attitude toward the church?

PERSONAL REFLECTION. How do you contribute to the unity or disunity of the church?

Many things divide Christians from other Christians—gifts, doctrine, church government, mode of baptism and so on. Whether we like it or not, divisions have occurred, and we must live with them. But we can be inspired and guided by Scriptures to do better. *Read Ephesians 4:1-16.*

---

1. Why are the qualities mentioned in verses 1-3 essential for unity in the church?

2. Christian unity must be built on a foundation of shared beliefs and experiences. What shared beliefs and experiences does Paul mention (vv. 4-6)?

How do these "ones" provide the foundation for unity?

3. What steps might you take to strengthen your own relationships within your church or fellowship?

4. Triumphant conquerors often gave gifts to their citizens. What "gifts" did Christ give the church when he ascended to heaven (vv. 7-11)?

5. What is the overall purpose of the gifts mentioned here?

6. One purpose of gifted church leaders is to equip or prepare God's people for service, that is, ministry (4:12). How does that compare with the way we often think about Christian ministers?

7. The Greek word translated "prepare" or "equip" (4:12) means to mend a net or set a broken bone. How does preparing/equipping enlarge your understanding of the way Christians are to live and work together?

8. In what areas do you feel prepared for service within your church or Christian community? Explain.

9. What dangers threaten an immature church (vv. 14-16)?

10. The Christian church in every generation must confront false "winds of teaching." What false teachings are we facing in our generation?

11. For the church to mature in Christ, members must "speak the truth in love." What can happen when truth is not spoken in love?

What happens when love is spoken without truth?

12. Paul uses the image of the body to describe the way the church should work together. What part of the body are you?

How can you do your part to build up the body in truth and love?

13. Summarize your understanding of essential elements of the church contained in this study and study 10.

Ask God to show you your place in the community and mission of the church.

Now or Later

The church can be described as a fellowship of the saved. Based on our previous studies concerning sanctification, the church could also be described as the fellowship of those who are being saved. Make a list of the ways in which the church has been used by God to shaped your character and aid your growth in salvation.

Read the following passages for further study and reflection on the nature and purpose of the church: Matthew 16:13-28; Acts 2:42-47; 1 Corinthians 6:1-13; 12:12-26; Philippians 4:1-9.

12

Hope for the Future

When I was a boy, my older brother used to get magazines that had futuristic drawings on the covers. Some magazines were science fiction; others were technical magazines about machines or cars. Whatever kind of magazine he bought, those cover illustrations had a mystical effect on me. They created an anxious hunger for the future, a hope for a glittering utopia of human civilization run by amazing machines. Now, some forty or more years later, I am still waiting for the "future." Granted, we have some amazing machines, but the dawning of utopia seems pretty far off. The Scriptures speak of the future, but its character and coming are different and far better than my childhood fantasies. This teaching about the future is called *eschatology*.

GROUP DISCUSSION. Every so often certain groups of Christians proclaim that they have figured out the secret of the time of the return of Jesus Christ. How do you respond to such teaching? Why does a reflection on the teaching of the last things inspire so much excitement?

PERSONAL REFLECTION. What are you most looking forward to about the Lord's return?

Glorification focuses on the personal condition of a believer on the other side of death. The study of eschatology is a consideration of the condition of the entire world when God completes his saving and restoring work of his fallen and rebellion creation. *Read 2 Peter 3:3-14.*

1. Looking over the whole passage, what are some things that the coming of the Lord involves?

2. We think of the last things as dealing with the future, but that is only part of it. How does the teaching on the last things look back to the past as well as to the future (vv. 1-7)?

3. Christians can expect to encounter scoffers in the "last days." What reasons do scoffers give for scoffing at the Lord's coming (vv. 3-4)?

4. Believers, too, are tempted to be discouraged and skeptical about the Lord's return. How have you handled such struggles?

5. Why would scoffers want to forget about the creation and the flood?

6. How can recalling the creation and the flood strengthen our faith in the Lord's return?

7. What frustrations and benefits arise from the way God measures time (vv. 8-9)?

8. What does Peter mean when he says, "the day of the Lord will come like a thief in the night" (v. 10)?

9. There are groups of people who say that Jesus has already secretly returned. Based on Peter's teaching, what can we say to them?

10. What will the coming judgment be like (vv. 7, 10)?

---

11. God will create a new heaven and earth in place of the old (vv. 10-13). How will life on earth be different than it is now?

---

12. Thinking about our hope for the future is much more than idle speculation. How can thinking about the future practically affect your way of thinking and acting (vv. 11-14)?

Ask God to help you face the challenges of today with a strong hope for his future.

Now or Later

Going outside onto a street at night you can easily have a sense that something is not quite safe. After Jesus returns, the world is restored and the curse is removed, it will be safe to go out anywhere, at any time. Try picturing yourself in a renewed world now. How do you respond to the idea of being in a world whether there is no more danger or pain?

Leader's Notes

MY GRACE IS SUFFICIENT FOR YOU. (2 COR 12:9)

Leading a Bible discussion can be an enjoyable and rewarding experience. But it can also be *scary*—especially if you've never done it before. If this is your feeling, you're in good company. When God asked Moses to lead the Israelites out of Egypt, he replied, "O Lord, please send someone else to do it"! (Ex 4:13). It was the same with Solomon, Jeremiah and Timothy, but God helped these people in spite of their weaknesses, and he will help you as well.

You don't need to be an expert on the Bible or a trained teacher to lead a Bible discussion. The idea behind these inductive studies is that the leader guides group members to discover for themselves what the Bible has to say. This method of learning will allow group members to remember much more of what is said than a lecture would.

These studies are designed to be led easily. As a matter of fact, the flow of questions through the passage from observation to interpretation to application is so natural that you may feel that the studies lead themselves. This study guide is also flexible. You can use it with a variety of groups—student, professional, neighborhood or church groups. Each study takes forty-five to sixty minutes in a group setting.

There are some important facts to know about group dynamics and encouraging discussion. The suggestions listed below should enable you to effectively and enjoyably fulfill your role as leader.

Preparing for the Study

1. Ask God to help you understand and apply the passage in your own life. Unless this happens, you will not be prepared to lead others. Pray too for the various members of the group. Ask God to open your hearts to the message of his Word and motivate you to action.

2. Read the introduction to the entire guide to get an overview of the entire book and the issues which will be explored.

3. As you begin each study, read and reread the assigned Bible passage to familiarize yourself with it.

4. This study guide is based on the New International Version of the Bible.

It will help you and the group if you use this translation as the basis for your study and discussion.

5. Carefully work through each question in the study. Spend time in meditation and reflection as you consider how to respond.

6. Write your thoughts and responses in the space provided in the study guide. This will help you to express your understanding of the passage clearly.

7. It might help to have a Bible dictionary handy. Use it to look up any unfamiliar words, names or places. (For additional help on how to study a passage, see chapter five of *Leading Bible Discussions*, InterVarsity Press.)

8. Consider how you can apply the Scripture to your life. Remember that the group will follow your lead in responding to the studies. They will not go any deeper than you do.

9. Once you have finished your own study of the passage, familiarize yourself with the leader's notes for the study you are leading. These are designed to help you in several ways. First, they tell you the purpose the study guide author had in mind when writing the study. Take time to think through how the study questions work together to accomplish that purpose. Second, the notes provide you with additional background information or suggestions on group dynamics for various questions. This information can be useful when people have difficulty understanding or answering a question. Third, the leader's notes can alert you to potential problems you may encounter during the study.

10. If you wish to remind yourself of anything mentioned in the leader's notes, make a note to yourself below that question in the study.

Leading the Study

1. Begin the study on time. Open with prayer, asking God to help the group to understand and apply the passage.

2. Be sure that everyone in your group has a study guide. Encourage the group to prepare beforehand for each discussion by reading the introduction to the guide and by working through the questions in the study.

3. At the beginning of your first time together, explain that these studies are meant to be discussions, not lectures. Encourage the members of the group to participate. However, do not put pressure on those who may be hesitant to speak during the first few sessions. You may want to suggest the following guidelines to your group.

☐ Stick to the topic being discussed.

☐ Your responses should be based on the verses which are the focus of the discussion and not on outside authorities such as commentaries or speakers.

☐ These studies focus on a particular passage of Scripture. Only rarely should you refer to other portions of the Bible. This allows for everyone to participate in in-depth study on equal ground.

☐ Anything said in the group is considered confidential and will not be discussed outside the group unless specific permission is given to do so.

☐ We will listen attentively to each other and provide time for each person present to talk.

☐ We will pray for each other.

4. Have a group member read the introduction at the beginning of the discussion.

5. Every session begins with a group discussion question. The question or activity is meant to be used before the passage is read. The question introduces the theme of the study and encourages group members to begin to open up. Encourage as many members as possible to participate, and be ready to get the discussion going with your own response.

This section is designed to reveal where our thoughts or feelings need to be transformed by Scripture. That is why it is especially important not to read the passage before the discussion question is asked. The passage will tend to color the honest reactions people would otherwise give because they are, of course, supposed to think the way the Bible does.

You may want to supplement the group discussion question with an ice-breaker to help people to get comfortable. See the community section of *Small Group Idea Book* for more ideas.

You also might want to use the personal reflection question with your group. Either allow a time of silence for people to respond individually or discuss it together.

6. Have a group member (or members if the passage is long) read aloud the passage to be studied. Then give people several minutes to read the passage again silently so that they can take it all in.

7. Question 1 will generally be an overview question designed to briefly survey the passage. Encourage the group to look at the whole passage, but try to avoid getting sidetracked by questions or issues that will be addressed later in the study.

8. As you ask the questions, keep in mind that they are designed to be used just as they are written. You may simply read them aloud. Or you may prefer to express them in your own words.

There may be times when it is appropriate to deviate from the study guide. For example, a question may have already been answered. If so, move on to the next question. Or someone may raise an important question not covered in the guide. Take time to discuss it, but try to keep the group from going off on tangents.

9. Avoid answering your own questions. If necessary, repeat or rephrase them until they are clearly understood. Or point out something you read in the leader's notes to clarify the context or meaning. An eager group quickly

becomes passive and silent if they think the leader will do most of the talking.

10. Don't be afraid of silence. People may need time to think about the question before formulating their answers.

11. Don't be content with just one answer. Ask, "What do the rest of you think?" or "Anything else?" until several people have given answers to the question.

12. Acknowledge all contributions. Try to be affirming whenever possible. Never reject an answer. If it is clearly off-base, ask, "Which verse led you to that conclusion?" or again, "What do the rest of you think?"

13. Don't expect every answer to be addressed to you, even though this will probably happen at first. As group members become more at ease, they will begin to truly interact with each other. This is one sign of healthy discussion.

14. Don't be afraid of controversy. It can be very stimulating. If you don't resolve an issue completely, don't be frustrated. Move on and keep it in mind for later. A subsequent study may solve the problem.

15. Periodically summarize what the group has said about the passage. This helps to draw together the various ideas mentioned and gives continuity to the study. But don't preach.

16. At the end of the Bible discussion you may want to allow group members a time of quiet to work on an idea under "Now or Later." Then discuss what you experienced. Or you may want to encourage group members to work on these ideas between meetings. Give an opportunity during the session for people to talk about what they are learning.

17. Conclude your time together with conversational prayer, adapting the prayer suggestion at the end of the study to your group. Ask for God's help in following through on the commitments you've made.

18. End on time.

Many more suggestions and helps are found in *Leading Bible Discussions*, which is part of the LifeGuide Bible Study series.

Components of Small Groups

A healthy small group should do more than study the Bible. There are four components to consider as you structure your time together.

Nurture. Small groups help us to grow in our knowledge and love of God. Bible study is the key to making this happen and is the foundation of your small group.

Community. Small groups are a great place to develop deep friendships with other Christians. Allow time for informal interaction before and after each study. Plan activities and games that will help you get to know each other. Spend time having fun together—going on a picnic or cooking dinner together.

Worship and prayer. Your study will be enhanced by spending time praising God together in prayer or song. Pray for each other's needs—and keep track of how God is answering prayer in your group. Ask God to help you to apply what you are learning in your study.

Outreach. Reaching out to others can be a practical way of applying what you are learning, and it will keep your group from becoming self-focused. Host a series of evangelistic discussions for your friends or neighbors. Clean up the yard of an elderly friend. Serve at a soup kitchen together, or spend a day working on a Habitat house.

Many more suggestions and helps in each of these areas are found in *Small Group Idea Book.* Information on building a small group can be found in *Small Group Leaders' Handbook* and *The Big Book on Small Groups* (both from Inter-Varsity Press). Reading through one of these books would be worth your time.

Study 1. God in the World & in the Word. Psalm 19.

Purpose: To heighten our awareness of the ways God is revealing himself to us.

Question 1. God reveals himself in creation and in Scripture. God's revelation in creation is called *general* revelation. God's revelation through the Scriptures is called *special* revelation. Psalm 19 describes both types of revelation: verses 1-6 are about general revelation, while verses 7-14 are about special revelation.

Question 2. When we view the world as a work of art, we are drawn to appreciate the beauty of the world and God's skill as the artist. Modern scientists were inclined to see the world as a vast machine, but in the late twentieth century, people were inclined to see the world as a living organism.

Question 3. In Romans 1:18-20 the apostle Paul says that God's power and divine nature are clearly seen through creation. The fact that religion is a worldwide phenomenon demonstrates that there is an inner awareness of a Creator to whom we owe worship and devotion.

Question 4. Creation declares God's glory, but it does not declare his name. Through creation we can know that he exists, but his personal character and offer of salvation through Jesus Christ can only be known through a special act of revelation. (See 2 Tim 3:15-17 for additional insights about special revelation.)

Question 5. Without the light and warmth of the sun there is no life. And so it is without God. As the sun's light penetrates everywhere, so there is nowhere that God is not present in his universe. The theological term for this is *omnipresence.* There are other comparisons between the sun and God; help your group think of them.

Question 8. We tend to think of laws as restraints and burdens, but notice the striking contrast with David. Help the group to think about what life would be like without human laws, and then what life would be like without divine laws.

Question 9. Here is the "rub" in knowing God. Because God is holy, we can't get close to him without sensing our moral responsibility and our sin. Only those who are willing to face their sin and their need to do something about it can approach God.

Question 10. This is an important question as you begin this series of studies. If we are going to study God and what Christians believe, then there must be a willingness to *act* on it. As James reminds us, "Do not merely listen to the word, and so deceive yourselves. Do what it says" (Jas 1:22).

Study 2. Knowing God. Isaiah 40:9-31.

Purpose: To find strength and comfort in the knowledge of God's sovereign power.

General note. In classical theology we consider what is called "theology proper," in which we consider the attributes of God. No definition is adequate to describe God. But as we see what he is like through his creation and care for his people, we come to know him better.

Question 1. If we find the study of God boring or dry, then we have missed something. The Scriptures and experiences show that God is glorious, beautiful, exciting and inspires awe in his people. The proper study of God, done in the right way, can only lead us to worship.

The ringing proclamation is that *God is here* and *God reigns*. We must believe these things in our hearts if we are to trust him. It is also important to note that God is proclaimed both as *Judge* and *Savior*. He brings judgment to the enemies of his people and gathers his people like a shepherd. The peace of Psalm 23 and the battle of the book of Revelation are both contained in these verses.

Question 2. These verses affirm that God *alone* is the creator of all things. No thing and no one existed before him or beside him. This is in contrast to polytheism, which believes there are many gods. It also contrasts with a belief called dualism, which teaches that there are two equal gods, one good, the other evil, that are in constant battle with one another. These verses also portray the *immensity* of God. He is not only before all things, he is "bigger than all things."

Question 3. These verses continue the reflection on the immensity of God. Isaiah also proclaims the *transcendence* of God (v. 17). God is not only bigger than all things, he above all things. In addition, these verses also show the *omnipotence* of God (v. 23). He is more powerful than anything or anyone else.

At the time Isaiah wrote this, Israel was about to be defeated and to have a large portion of its inhabitants deported to Babylon. The Israelites would fear that God was not with them anymore or that he was not as powerful as the god of Babylon. At that time each nation had its own national god. The power of its god was displayed by its victory over other nations. Isaiah tells Israel that their God is more than a mere "national god"; he is God over all nations. His power is not reflected in the defeat of Israel.

Question 5. Idols are primarily physical representations of what we supremely value. To find out if we have idols, we need merely ask what is most important to us and look at what we give most of our thought, energy and time to. Anything that comes before God is an idol—our possessions, relationships, studies, career ambitions and so on. Help people in the group reflect on the presence of other religions; perhaps you could pick up on the group discussion question.

Once a Greek philosopher wrote that "the proper study of man is man." For most of the twentieth century we could make a play on this and say, "The proper worship of man is man." However, as we enter into the early years of the twenty-first century there is a new religious awareness that again looks to spiritual realities. It is not a forgone conclusion that this religious awareness will lead to a revival of Christianity. It is a dangerously real possibility that new "idols" and gods will take captive the hearts of people.

Question 6. There is no way that we can adequately conceive of God. Both the wealthy and the poor fail in their attempts to portray God. But sadly, that doesn't stop us. There is a false notion that comes with idolatry. People believe that if they make an image and worship it, they will gain personal power and favor. One of humanity's fundamental drives is for power. We want to be in control. We believe that we can control what we can understand. If we can reduce God to an idol, then we can control him.

Question 7. The belief that God is an uninvolved creator is called *deism*. It became a popular form of religion during the Enlightenment. Although the term *deism* has fallen into disuse, its teachings have become a part of the way many people think about God.

Question 8. This question brings out into the open issues of classical theology that have been touched on so far only in the preceding leader's notes of this study.

Question 9. The struggle for spiritual reality is difficult. The root issue is this: Is God really with us; is he Emmanuel? Isaiah affirms that God is, in fact, with us. And for believers this is good news. With his presence comes strength and power. It is important to keep in mind that hope (v. 31) is not a passive waiting but a strong and eager anticipation.

Now or Later. Here are a few heresies or extremes to avoid when seeking to understand the attributes of God: pantheism—God is in everything and synonymous with all created things; unholiness—since God is all-powerful and sovereign, he is the cause of sin; impersonality—God is only energy and power, not a person; dualism—God and Satan are two equal but opposing forces.

Study 3. Jesus: God with Us. John 1:1-18.

Purpose: To grow in our gratitude to God for coming to us in Jesus Christ and making us his children.

General note. The study of Jesus is called *Christology.* It is usually divided into two parts: (1) his *person* (his deity and his humanity) and (2) his *work* (how he saves us). In this passage we get a glimpse of these two different aspects of Christology, although the primary focus is on his person. The work of Christ will be picked up in study 7 as we look at the doctrine of justification.

Question 1. William Temple writes, "The *Logos* [word] alike for Jew and Gentile represents the ruling fact of the universe, and represents that fact as the self-expression of God. The Jew will remember that 'by the Word of the Lord were the heavens made'; the Greek will think of the rational principle of which all natural laws are particular expressions. Both will agree that his logos is the starting-point of all things" (as quoted by Leon Morris in *The Gospel According to John,* The New International Commentary on the New Testament [Grand Rapids, Mich.: Eerdmans, 1971], p. 123).

Light and *life* also pick up themes about God from the Old Testament. The very first words of God in Genesis are, "Let there be light" (Gen 1:3). This idea is continued throughout the Scriptures: "For with you is the fountain of life; in your light we see light" (Ps 36:9).

Question 3. God is a mystery. Our limited minds must bow before the mystery of God as he chooses to reveal himself. The important thing to keep in mind as we seek to consider truths that are beyond our comprehension is that we must be faithful to the Scriptures as they make God known.

Question 4. The Word means that Christ is means of communication of God. In human communication we write words on pages. Divine communication is not only words on a page (Scripture) but also human flesh—*incarnation.* Only God has life in himself that is *self-generating.* Light not only refers to understanding but also stands in contrast to darkness. As light, Jesus is the essence of good that stands in opposition to evil.

Question 5. The wisdom of the early church was to seek to accept that which was revealed yet beyond their comprehension. Clearly the Scriptures teach that there is only one God (Ex 20:3; Deut 6:4). Clearly Jesus has the attributes of God; that is, he was present at creation with life in himself. They became aware that the Holy Spirit had the same attributes as well (see study 4). They came to the conclusion that there must be one God in three persons—the Trinity.

Question 6. There is battle implicit in his coming. He was not welcome in his world. Because God made all people in his image, the world should have recognized him when he came to them. After all, even children can recognize their parents.

Leon Morris suggests that verse 11 could be translated, "He came home." Because God made Israel "his own" and had been caring for them for over eighteen hundred years of Jewish history, they should have recognized him when he came in bodily form. The implicit resistance to God, that is, the presence of darkness, means that every generation has a choice to make. Christianity goes through periods of decay and revival because of this ongoing resistance.

Question 7. The greatest miracle of all is that the infinite, eternal, omnipotent, omniscient and omnipresent Creator could take on human flesh and become limited to one place and a human body. If you believe this, then walking water, turning water into wine or feeding five thousand people with a few loaves of bread and fish is hardly anything at all.

Question 8. John clearly affirms that Jesus existed as the second person of the Godhead before he was born! He was not promoted to godlike status because of the quality of his character.

Question 10. Someone once commented, "God has always had the disadvantage of being invisible." Until the coming of Christ, God made himself known without bodily form through his words and his actions. But in Christ God could be seen, heard and touched as never before (see 1 Jn 1:1).

> "While the New Testament sees God as the Father of all men [and women], paradoxically it does not think of all men as sons of God. God's attitude to all men is that of a Father. All are His sons in the sense that He made them. But men are His sons in the full sense only as they respond to what He does for them in Christ. When they receive the Word they are born again into the heavenly family" (Morris, *John*, p. 98).

Historical extremes to avoid regarding the character of Jesus Christ include Arianism: Jesus was created by God; *modalism:* there is one God revealed in three forms; *Docetism:* Jesus was not truly human, he just took on the appearance of humanity to communicate with us; *Apollinarianism:* Christ had a human body but divine soul; *monophysitism:* Christ had only one nature—divine; Christ's human body was somehow more "divine" than ours.

Study 4. The Holy Spirit. John 14:15-27.

Purpose: To grow in our responsiveness to the Spirit as he cares for us, counsels us and guides us.

General note. Historically the doctrine of the Holy Spirit is one of the least

developed of all Christian beliefs. This is one reason for the current controversy over the Spirit. The church, after two thousand years, is only beginning
to give the Spirit focused attention.

The Holy Spirit is God, a member of the Trinity with the Father and the
Son. His ministry is seen throughout both the Old and New Testaments. In
the Old Testament, however, his ministry was focused on national leaders,
prophets, priests and kings. In the New Testament every believer receives the
privileged anointing of the Spirit.

The Spirit's ministry in the church is rich and varied. He leads believers in
holiness, empowers gifts for ministry and equips the church to witness. There
are two important series of references to the Holy Spirit in the Gospel of John:
14:15-26 and 15:26—16:15.

Question 1. The teaching about the character of God in the Scriptures is
never abstract or speculative. You could say we learn about God on a "need to
know" basis. The disciples were in great need and Jesus reveals another
dimension of God that they had not heard about as he now begins to teach
them.

Question 2. The Greek word translated "Counselor" literally means "one
called alongside." It was used of lawyers who provided legal counsel in a
courtroom. However, the word in the New Testament refers not merely to a
legal counselor but to a friend, guide and teacher who helps us with personal
problems.

Question 3. The Holy Spirit is the secret gift that belongs only to the believer.
From the outside Christianity is sometimes seen as merely a series of activities and rituals. From the inside it is rich invisible fellowship connecting us
to God and each other.

Question 4. The Spirit is always speaking to his people. The real issue is, are
we willing to respond obediently to his guidance? After Jesus ascended to
heaven, his presence and ministry with the disciples could only be discerned
by spiritual perception.

We live in a materialistic and secular culture. We can easily be so preoccu-
pied with the physical aspects of life that we, in daily practice, forget all about
the spiritual. When this happens we have no sense of the Lord's presence.
The same is true on a broader scale when God is dismissed from public areas
of life such as education, government and the workplace. As we go about living our daily lives, God can seem irrelevant to the most pressing issues
around us.

The pace of life in the modern world is also a great hindrance to a responsive sense of the Spirit's presence. Like static on an old radio, there is often so
much going on that the voice of the Spirit never quite breaks through.

Question 5. In the Old Testament the work of the Holy Spirit was seen primarily through its ministry with prophets and rulers. They were anointed for

a specific ministry and often for a specific period of time. (Note that the Spirit came on Saul at specific times—for instance, 1 Sam 11:6. See also David's prayer in Ps 51:11 after he sinned with Bathsheba: "Do not . . . take your Holy Spirit from me.") However, in the messianic age brought by Jesus, the Spirit continues with God's people and goes far beyond ministry to the depths of intimacy in our hearts. Consequently the disciples need not worry that they are going to be left alone.

Question 6. We touch again on the mystery of the Trinity. For the Spirit to be present with the disciples means that Jesus will be present with them, even though he is leaving them to return to the Father. Although denominations have distinctives about Christian doctrine and ways of worship, at the center of the Christian church, which is true for all believers in all places and all times, is the teaching that Jesus is present by means of the Spirit. This means that there is a fundamental unity in the midst of diversity.

Question 7. "All things" (v. 26) probably means "everything you will need to know." One of the foundational principles of a healthy spiritual life is to remember what God has said and done. God was constantly calling Israel to remember his mighty acts and provisions for redemption. In contrast, Satan has an investment in taking the Word of God out of our hearts, minds and memories. God has provided the Holy Spirit to help us remember and therefore live in the spiritual truth of his Word. It is important to cultivate an attitude of listening to the Spirit and act on what we hear.

Question 8. Peace is often thought of as the absence of trouble. But in Christ it is more than that. It is a way of living ordered by God's love and power. Morris observes, "When the world uses 'Peace' in a greeting it expresses a hope. It can do no more. . . . But Christ effectually gives men peace" (Morris, *John,* p. 657). The peace of Jesus is the peace of his presence with us, the assurance that the Father loves us and that the Spirit is our constant companion. The world can only offer outward things that can never satisfy our souls and will pass away with time and death. The biblical meaning of *peace* is not merely personal but corporate. Peace is good relationships within a community of people. It is the different instruments playing in harmony in a symphony. This is the peace that Jesus brings his people by the Spirit.

Question 9. The Father, Son and Spirit together are active in the life of every believer. The Spirit teaches, reminds and brings peace. Jesus commands us as our Lord and the Father is continually the source of love toward us.

Question 10. Love, obedience and spiritual knowledge are inseparable. We obey Jesus not out of legalism but out of affection. God responds to affectionate obedience by taking up residence with us and revealing himself to us.

Throughout church history there have been those who declared that the Spirit freed them from obedience. It is actually the other way around. The Spirit frees us to obey. (We will look at this in more detail in study 8.)

Now or Later. Extremes to avoid when thinking about the Spirit: modalism—the Spirit is the same as the Father and the Son; impersonality—the Spirit is only the power of God, not actually God; reductionism—the Spirit is not as important as the Father and the Son.

Study 5. Our Identity & Dignity. Genesis 1:24—2:25.

Purpose: To discover the source of our identity and dignity as people made in the image of God.

General note. The biblical study of human nature begins in Genesis 1—3. The rest of Scripture can only be understood in light of these chapters. Every other reference to humanity in the Scriptures merely reflects the truths recorded in Genesis. One theme normally included in the biblical study of humanity is the role of work. God made us and blessed us with the responsibility to care for the creation. There is no question in the study that explicitly addresses this topic. But as the leader you might raise the issue if there is time.

Question 1. Created on the sixth day, we humans are animals. If we deny this, we miss something true about our nature. But this is not to say that we are merely "naked apes." We are also made in the image of God. He has made us vice regents over creation. We are responsible to God to care for and cultivate the world. Like God, who created the world, we have the ability to create and shape our environment.

Question 2. In the first chapter it is clear that humans are part of the creation, made along with other animals on the sixth day. In the second chapter humans are the crown of creation. God shapes and molds the world to meet the special needs of the human race. The latter account is like a zoom lens, focusing much more closely and specifically on humanity. To say that these two chapters contain two separate accounts is to miss the Hebrew style of communication. Truths are stated in one way and then rephrased from a slightly different angle. A cursory reading of the book of Proverbs or Psalms can clearly illustrate this.

Question 3. God is intimately involved in Adam's life, much like a parent with his child. He gives Adam a carefully prescribed place to live, and he notices his need for companionship. He gives Adam a great deal of freedom, along with responsibility to care for the Garden. God is so involved that he is even interested in the names Adam gives the animals.

Question 4. Adam had a personal relationship with God, and from the Creator he learned to live and love. What emptiness he would have faced without that relationship. Adam would also be an image-bearer without an image to reflect. He learned to be a caretaker of the Garden because he had seen God care for him. He knew what it was to be *a* person because he had seen *the* Person. Without God, Adam would have missed the sense of dignity and responsibility bestowed on him as a divine gift.

Question 5. Adam knew his own dignity because he was in contact with God. We too need to spend enough time in the presence of God that we know our own dignity.

Question 6. Although Adam was made in the image of God, he was not God. He was subject to God. The tree would help Adam keep his responsibility to God in perspective. Adam would learn that God requires obedience.

Question 7. Most people think of restraints as infringements. In reality God's restraints are reminders of what is true about us. Remember that our identity and dignity are bestowed by God. If we break away from him, we lose our dignity and identity.

Question 9. Adam and Eve's relationship can be described as mutual companionship and shared responsibility. In Genesis 1:28 the mandate to subdue the earth (called the cultural mandate) is given to both the man and the woman. Adam finds the fulfillment of his whole person in Eve. She shares his nature. Likewise, Eve derives her nature from Adam and participates with him in the image of God. Neither one could declare independence from the other without personally losing something essential.

It is striking that God made the human race so that we have need of human companionship. God never intended his relationship with us to exclude the need or desire for other people. Human relationship is the very essence of the image of God, according to Genesis 1:26-27. God made humanity in his image, "male and female he created them."

Question 10. Loneliness is one of the worst causes of human suffering. Much of the sufferings of life and much of the risks of life can be faced if we feel we are not alone. Spiritual and emotional health are marked by the ability to be in relationship with other people.

Question 11. We need a balanced life. We need God, each other and the world we live in. To deny any one area, or to major on only one, is unhealthy.

Study 6. Our Identity & Depravity. Genesis 3.

Purpose: To consider the effects of sin and look to God for deliverance.

General note. This chapter describes the nature of sin and temptation. At its root, sin is challenging the character and intentions of God. Every sin committed since the original one is only a reflection of its evil.

Question 1. For some people this question will really help them experience the passage. Others can learn from their creative answers.

Question 2. Satan portrays God as an insecure tyrant, seeking to guard his position of power. Satan makes God's prohibition sound like something petty rather than something intended for human good.

Question 3. As an angel of light, Satan can make anything appear to be good. It is his nature to take a truth and twist it—even to the point of quoting Scripture, as he did with Jesus (see Mt 4:1-11). Like Eve and Jesus, we can be placed in situations—"setups"—that appeal to our weaknesses and lead us to choose disobedience and self-will over and against the purposes of God.

Question 4. This is a speculative question, but it is worth thinking about. It is possible that Adam and Eve were only thinking about the pleasure they derived from eating the food. Often the worst sins are committed with no sense of evil or wrongdoing at the time we are sinning. Only later, when the consequences appear, do we really think about the terrible thing we have done.

Question 5. Their nakedness was a physical symbol of their innocence. After they sinned, they could not stand to be naked because they now had something to hide—internally as well as externally. There is an intimate relationship between spiritual sin and physical needs. Sin has physical consequences, and Adam and Eve were responding to their guilt and shame by seeking a way to physically cover themselves.

Question 7. One of the ways we hide is to keep busy. We are too busy to pray, too busy to read Scripture, too busy to worship. A little inward reflection will reveal that we are frequently too busy because we don't want to pray, read Scripture or worship. We can even be so busy for God doing ministry in the church that we avoid time alone with God.

Question 9. All of creation, which was to be responsive to humanity, now becomes resistant. Childbearing and work, which were intended by God as sources of continual pleasure, now become strife-filled chores.

Question 10. Genesis 3:15 is referred to as the *protevangelium*, the first hint of the gospel. It is taken to imply that an offspring of a woman (Mary) will eventually confront the destructive work of Satan. While Satan will "bruise his heel"— that is, inflict damage on Jesus—in the end Jesus will triumph as Redeemer.

Question 11. Adam and Eve needed to cover their sin. God provided the covering with animal skins. Some see the skins as sacrifices God made on our behalf. Those sacrifices, it is suggested, are precursors of the death of Christ, who was sacrificed to cover our sin.

Question 12. In Alcoholics Anonymous, recovering alcoholics attend a meeting every week. They stand up before the people in the meeting, say their names and affirm, "I am an alcoholic." Their admission and public confession are essential for their continued sobriety. It might be helpful for Christians to do the same thing. We need to affirm and confess that we are sinful. When we confess our sinfulness to each other, we find strength and courage to face it.

Study 7. Deliverance from Sin. Romans 3:9-31.

Purpose: To appreciate what God has done in Christ to deliver us from our sinfulness back into fellowship with him.

General note. This study and the two that follow look at the way God saves us from sin. Our salvation has three parts: (1) We *were saved* when we accepted Christ, which is called *justification* (study 7); (2) we *are being saved,* which is called *sanctification* (study 8); and (3) we *shall be saved,* which is called *glorification* (study 9). The doctrine of justification by faith looks at how God delivers us from sin through the death of Jesus Christ. Martin Luther's grasp of this doctrine allowed him to expose the false religious merit system of medieval Christianity. The heart of the doctrine of justification may be remembered by the phrase "just as if I'd never sinned."

Question 1. Verse 11 is a key to this passage: "There is . . . no one who seeks God." In this relativistic age we want to believe that anyone who is sincere can approach God. But such thinking does not take sin seriously enough. We are all accountable to God, and none of us measures up.

Question 2. Sin is pervasive. Every part of our being is polluted by sin. However, this is not the same as being totally bad. We also have human dignity. Godet comments on the passage: "The throat is compared to a sepulchre; this refers to the language of the gross and brutal man, of whom it is said in common parlance, it seems as if he would like to eat you. The characteristic which follows contrasts with the former; it is the sugared tongue, which charms you like a melodious instrument" (as quoted by John Murray, *The Epistle to the Romans,* The New International Commentary on the New Testament [Grand Rapids, Mich.: Eerdmans, 1965], p. 104).

Question 3. We prefer to define sin as merely outward acts rather than as inward spiritual disobedience. To make matters worse, we find ways to hide our disobedience—helping at church, doing good works in the community and so on—as means to serve God on our own terms rather than his.

Question 4. This was the mistake of the leaders of Jesus' day and of those who continued to oppose Christianity. The Jewish leaders had managed to deceive themselves about the depth of sin in their hearts.

Question 5. These verses describe the wonderful work of God in justification. God removed the guilt of our sin freely (v. 24) by grace (v. 24) through faith in Jesus Christ (v. 22). We are made righteous not because of what we have done but because of what Jesus has done for us. God's part was to provide Jesus as the sacrifice for our sin. Our part is to receive his righteousness by faith.

Question 6. Verses 24-25 contain some of the most difficult theological concepts in the Bible. I have tried to work through them a question at a time. It might be good for you to look at a commentary or two on this passage. I suggest the *Wycliffe Bible Commentary* (Moody Press) or the *Eerdmans Bible Com-*

mentary (Eerdmans). The actions God has taken are (1) to freely justify us and (2) to provide redemption through Christ as a sacrifice of atonement.

Question 7. The word *justify* is a legal term which means to "declare not guilty." While borrowed from the legal system, it goes far beyond what any human court can do. A human court may extend mercy to someone who has been found guilty. But no human court may actually declare a defendant not guilty after he or she has been convicted of a crime. Yet this is exactly what God has done for us. However, God is not just "letting us off." A judge who simply let guilty people go free would be considered unjust. In Jesus the demands of the law were fully satisfied. Therefore, God can be both "just and the one who justifies those who have faith in Jesus" (v. 26).

Because we are justified, we don't have to live in fear of God. In fact, we can enjoy him. We can also experience a new pleasure in life. Psychological studies attribute a large number of mental disorders to guilt feelings. With the root of human guilt removed, there can be deliverance from such inward discomfort.

Question 8. The word *redemption* was borrowed from the slave market. It means "to pay a price to buy someone from slavery." We were slaves to sin, trapped in our addiction to disobedience. One way that redemption from sin should manifest itself is in a genuine desire to come to God. We should find that we want to worship God and that devotion to him comes more naturally. Hunger for Scripture and a desire to be with God's people are also natural after deliverance from the bondage of sin.

Question 9. On the one hand, it should humble us and fill us with pain that the Son of God had to die for us. On the other hand, it should be a tremendous relief—like being delivered from a debt that was far greater than we could pay. The meaning behind the words "sacrifice of atonement" is that God's wrath was satisfied through the death of a sacrificial victim. In the Old Testament, the victims were animals. In the New Testament, the one and only sacrificial victim is Jesus Christ. Don't be afraid to let the group struggle with the fact that God is angry with those who sin.

Question 10. Human pride is the root of sin. It is the reason why "no one . . . seeks God" (v. 11). The righteousness from God is a free gift and not something we can claim as our own.

Study 8. Freedom to Be Holy. Romans 8:1-17.

Purpose: To encourage dependence on the Spirit as we live holy lives.

General note. In Christian theology the subject of this study is called *sanctification*. After God declares us righteous (which we looked at in the previous study on justification), we must live righteous lives. In sanctification we face day-to-day issues of living out our salvation.

Christian holiness is a paradox. Although we are freed from the slavery to sin, we still struggle with sin. Although the Spirit leads us toward holiness, the sinful nature tries to pull us back. Although we have been given life, we must flee death.

Question 1. Paul declares that we have been delivered from condemnation, freed from the law of sin and death, given the gift of the Spirit and enabled to fulfill the law through the power of the Spirit. The core problems of humanity are addressed in these verses.

Question 2. Condemnation leaves us in a state of spiritual paralysis. Once we have been delivered from the condemnation of sin, we can have hope as we wrestle with the power of sin. And because we are no longer condemned by God, there is a whole new realm of the Spirit into which we can enter, in which there is not only grace but also power.

Question 3. God the Father sends the Son, the Son becomes our sin offering, and the Spirit indwells us with presence and power.

Question 4. Notice Paul's contrasts: those who live according to the sinful nature or Spirit (1) have their *minds* set according to the sinful nature or Spirit (v. 5), (2) do not or do *submit* to God's law (vv. 4, 7), (3) experience *death* or *life and peace* (v. 6). All those in Christ have both the Holy Spirit and, therefore, the power to live holy lives.

Question 5. Some members of the group may be discouraged by Paul's description. It is important to realize that Paul's portrait of the Christian is based on the overall pattern of a person's life, not an isolated moment. Until Christ returns, we will all have lapses into sin. However, because of the presence of the Spirit our lives should be increasingly characterized by righteousness. Before we had the Spirit, we were powerless to do anything but choose sin—we were slaves to sin. But now that we have the Spirit we have the freedom to choose *not* to sin. Whenever we choose to obey the Lord, we are living out our freedom.

Question 6. Old habit patterns of thought have to be replaced with new ones. Consider how you have thought "Christianly" about your lives. We must educate our minds to think properly. This also includes our actions and attitudes. Later on in Romans 12:1-2 the apostle will call us not to be conformed to the world but transformed by the renewing of our minds.

Question 7. Richard Foster writes, "Will power will never succeed in dealing with the deeply ingrained habits of sin." Quoting Emmet Fox he says, "As soon as you resist mentally any undesirable or unwanted circumstance, you thereby endow it with more power—power which it will use against you" (*Celebration of Discipline* [San Francisco: Harper & Row, 1978], p. 4). If we deceive ourselves into thinking we can overcome sin by sheer willpower, we will be trapped in self-dependence rather than relying on the grace of God. In contrast, by setting our minds on the Spirit we allow God to work through us to change our patterns of thoughts and actions.

Question 8. First, we need to expect a tension, even a struggle, within us as we seek to follow the Lord. In the words of John White's book *The Fight*, the Christian life *is a fight*. Our struggle is both outward and inward. Just knowing that removes confusion and opens the way for strength. Second, we are given hope. One day Christ will give life to our bodies. That hope is a source of strength and power—as a runner finds reserves of energy he didn't think he had as he dashes toward the finish line.

Question 9. We must choose not to sin, and we must be responsive to the promptings of the Spirit. The Spirit will guide and prompt us to live righteously.

Question 11. Perhaps part of our quiet time should be spent cultivating a listening heart. That will help us to be responsive to the Spirit as he convicts us of sinful actions or attitudes. We can also expect the Spirit to lead us into times of devotion to the Father.

Study 9. The Best Is Yet to Come. Romans 8:18-39.

Purpose: To realize that the suffering of this present age is merely a prelude to a glorious future.

General note. The final stage of our salvation is *glorification*. God will one day complete his work in us and the rest of creation. We will be fully renewed in the image of Christ, we will have resurrection bodies, and we will live in a re-created heaven and earth with Christ forever.

Question 1. Life is full of struggles. Paul uses the metaphors of slavery, childbirth and adoption to portray the battles we face in life.

Question 2. Our hope of glory can strengthen us to keep on resisting sin and live in holiness. Runners who have hope of finishing continue to run. Runners who have no hope drop out of the race.

Question 3. Waiting, in the Christian sense, is both an active and a passive experience. Our waiting is to be characterized by a strong sense of anticipation. (See Mt 25 and the parables about being ready for Christ's return.) But while we wait in anticipation, we are not to be demanding or angry with God for not coming according to our timetable. We wait in patient humility for the time when he is ready to complete his work.

Question 4. In verse 22 Paul spoke of creation groaning; in verse 23 he said we ourselves groan inwardly. Here he makes the startling claim that the Spirit groans in prayer to God on our behalf. It is comforting to know that the Spirit is constantly praying for us, especially since we don't know how to properly pray for ourselves and others.

Question 5. God's purpose is to make us like his Son, who fully reflects his image.

Question 6. We must admit that we are dealing with a mystery here. Scripture teaches two things that Christians are to affirm. The first is that God is Lord of all, and nothing happens without his knowledge and guidance. Second, Scripture is clear that God is not the author of evil. It is not clear how these two truths fit together. Nevertheless, it is important to make the distinction. God never asks us to be glad about bad things that happen to us. He calls us to look for his redeeming hand, even in the bad things, believing that his good purpose will somehow be accomplished. As believers we can take comfort that God is in control of our lives and that nothing that happens to us is not being used by him to make us like Jesus.

Question 8. God has given his Son's life for our life. If he has done that, then we can be assured that nothing is more important to God than our salvation.

Question 9. When bad things happen to us, we are sometimes tempted to question God's love. Paul doesn't deny that such things will happen, but he gives us strong assurance that they cannot separate us from God's love.

Questions 10-11. You might want to refer back to the two preceding studies to help the group with these questions. They both bring out clearly what has been implicit in the preceding studies about the classic theological understanding of the process of salvation. Although this process has been mentioned in the leader's notes, these questions invite the whole group to articulate and summarize their understanding of this process.

Study 10. The Mission of the Church. Acts 2.
Purpose: To encourage participation in the mission and fellowship of the church.

General note. This study and study 11 are on the church. The church consists of all who call on the name of Jesus Christ. However, Christians throughout the ages have spoken of the *visible* and the *invisible* church. The visible church is the organized church that exists on earth. The invisible church is the church both on earth and in heaven. It is the church as God sees it.

Question 1. The entire world mission of the church is glimpsed during the coming of the Spirit on the day of Pentecost. He enabled the church to speak across language barriers with the universal gospel. The Spirit is sent by the Son so the church has a message to proclaim. The Father has raised the Son from the dead so that the faith of the church is a living faith.

Question 2. The church was able to grow and expand around the world because it was not tied into one culture or one geographical place. Perhaps the revolutionary nature of the church that enabled it to spread is seen when it is placed in contrast to Judaism which was, at the time of Jesus, tied both to the land of Israel and to Jewish culture.

Question 3. The prophet Joel spoke of the last days, which began with the outpouring of the Spirit on Pentecost. According to Joel, the Spirit is given to all God's people under the new covenant, regardless of age, sex or social status. Under the old covenant, the Spirit was given primarily to prophets, priests and kings of Israel. Although God intended the church to be transcultural, Christians had a hard time understanding this. It required persecution from authorities, which forced the church out of Jerusalem (see Acts 4—7), a vision to Peter (Acts 9—10), and the raising up of those specially called to spread the word (Acts 13—18.). Even today Christians tend to view their own experience and traditions as the standard against which all must conform.

Question 5. In this first evangelistic message of the church, Peter covers the essentials of the gospel. He says that Jesus should be received as the Messiah of Israel because of (1) the quality of Jesus' life, which was attested by his miracles, (2) Jesus' resurrection from the dead (everyone in Jerusalem would have known that the tomb was empty), (3) David's psalm about resurrection, which couldn't have been about David because he was obviously dead, and (4) the outpouring of the Holy Spirit, which was a sign that Jesus had ascended to heaven and had triumphed over his enemies in fulfillment of Psalm 110.

Question 6. Peter was not afraid to point out guilt ("whom you crucified") or call for a response ("repent and believe"). Remember that many of the people there would have heard about the empty tomb. They would also have heard the message proclaimed to them with the power of the Holy Spirit. Many in our culture have dismissed the gospel message as unworkable and outdated. But freedom from guilt feelings, loss of purpose and unsatisfied spiritual hunger can only truly be met in the gospel. The Holy Spirit created a context in which the gospel could be heard in Jerusalem. He can and is doing the same thing today.

Question 8. This passage is the most succinct and comprehensive summary of the ministry of the church. Teaching, fellowship, breaking of bread, praying and performing signs before the world are basic to the ministry of the church.

Question 9. To break bread together in a home was an expression of intimacy. We need regular small gatherings of believers where there can be a shared experience of intimacy. Small groups that gather in homes or in dorms on campus can meet this need today. However, meeting together in small, intimate groups needs to be balanced with larger corporate worship. Our faith is strengthened and worship is enhanced when we gather with a larger number of believers in a public place.

Question 10. God commands us to spread the gospel. But our evangelizing is only the instrument, not the cause, of anyone's conversion. True conversion is always a result of the Holy Spirit.

Question 11. If we believe that conversions are primarily up to us, we will be driven to manipulate people into accepting Christ. Further, we will feel guilt if we aren't evangelizing every moment of the day. On the other hand, if we believe that our role in evangelism is insignificant, then we can become passive and apathetic about seeking opportunities to share the gospel.

Study 11. The Community of the Church. Ephesians 4:1-16.

Purpose: To encourage community, spiritual leadership and servanthood within the church.

General note. The Lord provides resources for the church. A set of beliefs, his presence and gifted people are essential means by which the church lives. One of the important but controversial areas of the church is church government. Should the church be run by an Episcopal, Presbyterian or Congregational form of government? Sincere and godly believers have taken different positions. In this passage we look at government of the church, not by organizational structures but spiritually gifted leaders.

Question 1. Humility, meekness, gentleness and patience are not qualities known for helping one succeed in most pursuits of life. On the other hand, Christian community cannot work unless these qualities are present. Christian character is the foundation of healthy church life.

Question 2. The foundational reason Christians gather as a church is the common beliefs we have about God. If we don't share common beliefs, then division must follow. If we forget our foundational beliefs, and we allow ourselves to be taken up with secondary matters, division is sure to follow.

Question 3. Although unity in the church is a gift of the Holy Spirit, that unity must be treasured and cultivated by our intentional response. Carelessness and neglect destroy the unity the Spirit provides.

Question 4. The gifts Christ gave the church (v. 11) are not abilities in the abstract, but gifted *people.* Such people are an essential means by which Jesus governs his church. If we allow ourselves to look at the gifts or the people who have them, we will miss the presence of Jesus as he leads us. The gifted people mentioned are apostles, prophets and pastor-teachers. Each plays a role in life of the church. Apostles were those who established churches, planting them in new places. Prophets are given to speak God's word and call God's people to turn from worldliness. Pastor-teachers are those who have the day-to-day responsibility of caring for needs and instructing people from the Scriptures.

Question 6. We come to know God and receive the fullness of his blessings by means of his gifts and gifted people. We need to pay attention to this because we can easily think that a new program or a better building is all that we need.

Question 7. Christian ministers are often viewed as professional Christians hired to do the ministry of the church. Paul states that the primary function of such people is to equip *God's people* (the so-called laity) to do the ministry of the church. Unfortunately, many churches and professional ministers have deviated from God's intention.

Question 8. Some people may not be able to identify areas in which they feel equipped for service. It is affirming for such people to hear how they have helped various members of the group.

Question 9. An immature church is blown about by a variety of doctrines. Mature believers know when it is best to "take a stand" on certain issues and when it is better to agree to disagree.

Question 10. Current false winds of doctrine include a lack of concern for Christian doctrine, a low view of Scripture, a self-centered prosperity gospel that makes us blind to the Spirit, an inadequate concern with gifts and the Holy Spirit (either too much emphasis or a complete disregard of the Spirit's ministry).

Question 11. Speaking the truth without love may be destructive. It can be a means of power or control over people with whom we disagree. However, loving people without speaking the truth may allow friends we care for to continue in error, which can also be destructive.

Study 12. Hope for the Future. 2 Peter 3:3-14.

Purpose: To find strength for living by looking for the return of Jesus Christ.

General note. The study of the "last things" in Christian theology is called *eschatology.* Central to Christian belief is the view that history will culminate in the coming of Jesus. At that time, God will judge the disobedient and vindicate the righteous (see Mt 25:31-46). A Christian's hope for the future is not merely for personal vindication and deliverance but for the judgment and restoration of all of creation (see Rev 21).

Question 2. It is principle of biblical interpretation that we look back in order to look forward. This reason for this is that God's work is consistent. When we look back in history we see that God has judged the world for sin. It is not surprising then to expect that at the conclusion of history, we know that God will again judge the world for sin.

Question 3. We are affected by those we associate with, especially when they care nothing about whether Jesus is coming back. Rather than consciously doubting the Lord's return, we are tempted to let the issue slip into relative unimportance in the way we think and live.

Question 4. Give the group time to talk here. It is important for people to share their doubts. Remind the group that there is a difference between doubting and scoffing. Doubting is a struggle to believe. Scoffing is a choice not to believe.

Question 5. Those who choose not to believe certainly don't want to acknowledge the fact that God judged disobedience in the past and will do so again in the future. Unbelief and scoffing are moral choices, not merely intellectual positions. God has called people to faith, and those who don't believe make deliberate, even if unconscious, choices not to believe.

Question 6. God has acted repeatedly in his world. There are times when we feel he is distant and uninvolved. By reflecting on what he has done in the past, we can have hope for the future.

Question 7. God doesn't measure time by human standards. We must adjust ourselves to his ways of time and not expect him to live by ours. Like an impatient child on a trip, we must wait. We can't hurry God by constantly asking, "Is it time yet?"

Question 8. A thief comes unexpectedly. Those who scoff will be completely surprised when the final day appears.

Question 9. Jesus' return may be unexpected, but it will not be secret. This is the point of Jesus' teaching in the Olivet Discourse (Mt 24:26-31).

Question 11. One major result of the purification of the world will be the absence of evil and sin. We can hardly imagine a pure world. What would it be like to go on a walk at any time of day or night and never have the slightest fear? What would it be like to enter into any relationship and never have to be cautious or guarded?

Question 12. We must never underestimate the power of hope. Hope for deliverance and vindication can keep us going in the hardest situations. We must not hope simply for a change in our personal circumstances but for a purifying judgment of God's creation. Encourage the group to think about such issues as personal goals, career, the way they use money, the social groups they associate with and so on.

Stephen D. Eyre is the pastor for ministry support and Christian discipleship at College Hill Presbyterian Church, Cincinnati, Ohio. He is coauthor with his wife, Jacalyn, of the Lifeguide Bible Study Matthew, *and the author of the LifeGuides* Deuteronomy *and* Jeremiah. *He has also written* Drawing Close to God: The Essentials of a Dynamic Quiet Time. *Someday he plans to retire to France and write full time.*

For Further Reading

Scripture
Sproul, R. C. *Knowing Scripture*. Downers Grove, Ill.: InterVarsity Press, 1977.
Stott, John R. W. *The Authority of the Bible*. Downers Grove, Ill.: InterVarsity Press, 1974.

God
Packer, J. I. *Knowing God*. Downers Grove, Ill.: InterVarsity Press, 1973.
Ramachandra, Vinoth. *Gods that Fail*. Downers Grove, Ill.: InterVarsity Press, 1996.

Jesus
Wright, N. T. *The Challenge of Jesus*. Downers Grove, Ill.: InterVarsity Press, 1999.
Wright, Christopher J. H. *Knowing Jesus Through the Old Testament*. Downers Grove, Ill.: InterVarsity Press, 1992.

The Holy Spirit
Ferguson, Sinclair. *The Holy Spirit*. Downers Grove, Ill.: InterVarsity Press, 1996.
Hummel, Charles E. *Fire in the Fireplace*. Downers Grove, Ill.: InterVarsity Press, 1993.

Human Nature
Macaulay, Ranald, and Jerram Barrs. *Being Human*. Downers Grove, Ill.: InterVarsity Press, 1978.
Sherlock, Charles. *The Doctrine of Humanity*. Downers Grove, Ill.: InterVarsity Press, 1996.

Sin
Plantinga, Cornelius, Jr. *Not the Way It's Supposed to Be: A Breviary of Sin*. Grand Rapids, Mich.: Eerdmans, 1995.

Redemption
Morris, Leon. *The Atonement*. Downers Grove, Ill.: InterVarsity Press, 1983.
Stott, John R. W. *The Cross of Christ*. Downers Grove, Ill.: InterVarsity Press, 1986.

Eternal Hope

Connelly, Douglas. *The Promise of Heaven*. Downers Grove, Ill.: InterVarsity Press, 2000.

Spiritual Growth

Smith, Gordon T. *Courage & Calling*. Downers Grove, Ill.: InterVarsity Press, 1999.

Lovelace, Richard F. *Dynamics of Spiritual Life*. Downers Grove, Ill.: InterVarsity Press, 1979.

Mulholland, M. Robert, Jr. *Invitation to a Journey*. Downers Grove, Ill.: InterVarsity Press, 1993.

Outreach

Pippert, Rebecca Manley. *Out of the Saltshaker*, Rev. Ed. Downers Grove, Ill.: InterVarsity Press, 1999.

Borthwick, Paul. *Six Dangerous Questions to Transform Your View of the World*. Downers Grove, Ill.: InterVarsity Press, 1996.

The Church

Snyder, Howard A. *The Community of the King*. Downers Grove, Ill.: InterVarsity Press, 1977.

Gibbs, Eddie. *ChurchNext*. Downers Grove, Ill.: InterVarsity Press, 2000.

End Times

Grenz, Stanley J. *The Millennial Maze*. Downers Grove, Ill.: InterVarsity Press, 1992.

Oropeza, B. J. *99 Reasons Why No One Knows When Christ Will Return*. Downers Grove, Ill.: InterVarsity Press, 1994.